BESAYDOO

BESAYDOO

poems

YALIE SAWEDA KAMARA

Jake Adam York Prize | Selected by Amaud Jamaul Johnson

MILKWEED EDITIONS

Published 2024 by Milkweed Editions
Printed in the United States of America
Cover design by Mary Austin Speaker
Author photo by JP Leong
24 25 26 27 28   5 4 3 2 1
First Edition

Library of Congress Cataloging-in-Publication Data

Names: Kamara, Yalie, author.
Title: Besaydoo : poems / Yalie Saweda Kamara ; selected by Amaud Jamaul Johnson.
Description: First edition. | Minneapolis : Milkweed Editions, 2024. | Summary: "Selected by Amaud Jamaul Johnson for the 2023 Jake Adam York Prize, Yalie Saweda Kamara's Besaydoo is an elegantly wrought love song to home-as place, as people, as body, and as language"-- Provided by publisher.
Identifiers: LCCN 2023019223 (print) | LCCN 2023019224 (ebook) | ISBN 9781639550319 (trade paperback) | ISBN 9781639550302 (ebook)
Subjects: LCGFT: Poetry.
Classification: LCC PS3611.A46475 B47 2024 (print) | LCC PS3611.A46475 (ebook) | DDC 811/.6--dc23/eng/20230711
LC record available at https://lccn.loc.gov/2023019223
LC ebook record available at https://lccn.loc.gov/2023019224

Milkweed Editions is committed to ecological stewardship. We strive to align our book production practices with this principle, and to reduce the impact of our operations in the environment. We are a member of the Green Press Initiative, a nonprofit coalition of publishers, manufacturers, and authors working to protect the world's endangered forests and conserve natural resources. *Besaydoo* was printed on acid-free 100% postconsumer-waste paper by Sheridan Saline, Inc.

This book is lovingly dedicated to my mother, Agatha Kamara, who braved ocean, uncertainty, and nightfall so that I could speak. Thank you. May you hear your voice in mine.

CONTENTS

"HAN GO. HAN KAM."

—Sierra Leonean Krio Proverb

"THE HELPING HAND THAT LEAVES IN LOVE RETURNS IN LOYALTY."

BESAYDOO

OAKLAND AS HOME, HOME AS MYTH
for my sister, Chanel Selestok

Oakland is a killing field, they say.

But what about the fragrance of candy in public places and how
autumn waits tight-lipped while summer slowly stretches its limbs

like a tired infant? The upper level of the MacArthur BART Station
smells like Palmer's Cocoa Butter because being ashy in The Town

is worse than jaywalking. The aroma of chocolate blankets the opposing
platforms, while warm air kisses bare ankles and calves. Folks are ready

to flex for this last bit of summer. October, here, is like July almost anywhere else.

Oakland is a killing field, they say.

But what if, in this story of trickling blood, there is no gun, but instead a finger
pricked by a blackberry bush on Thornhill Drive? And what if the sting

is forgiven when the fruit's tangy juice launches itself across the endpoints of
our mouths like a shooting star at the horizon of Skyline Boulevard?

Sometimes, pain in Oakland comes from foraging through a thicket of joy.

Oakland is a killing field, they say.

But what about ritual rising from downtown's liquid belly? Amoeba-shaped
Lake Merritt is the largest, man-made body of water in America. No

native in the last fifty years has lived to tell about happily swimming in its murky brown
pool, for we know better: we show our love from the shores. You'll find

us sitting cross-legged either sharing office break secrets or watching our
babies tangle in the verdant grass blades of the lake's banks.

Lake Merritt is a confessional booth: we release our fears and secrets
into the mouth of algae hungering to filter any wisdom from our chaos.

We show gratitude in return, crafting an air-shaped haiku at the water's edge:

> The Town pilgrimage:
> Exchange worry for hope and
> Wash away madness.

Oakland is a killing field they say.
But what about Raphael Saadiq's voice, and how it coaxes the fog to burn invisibly?
Or the silver-haired stranger who makes a paper plane with a little boy he just met

at the Fruitvale BART Station and then teaches him how to mischievously fly it down
the 54 bus's narrow aisle?

What about our Michelin food rating surveys? The way we walk slowly past Mexican,
Ethiopian, and Korean eateries just to make sure that the food is good enough for Mexican,
Ethiopian, and Korean folks to eat there, too.

Oakland is a killing field, they say.
Oakland is a killing field, maybe, they say.

Most outsiders quietly confess to not knowing which is better: to approach The Town
with a fistful of flowers or a frame covered by a bulletproof vest. They fidget while

we walk past, the keys to The Town's front door jingling in our pocket. Wise, sassy,
fickle, and human: we are the bucktoothed city that made you wish you never wore braces.

Land of dirty concrete and sunshine. Land of the slain and the ever rising. Land of
Tom Hanks and bullets. Land of Sideshows and Market Hall. Land of Chow Mein and
pine trees. It's true, our contradiction is dizzying.

We fall and get back up again and tell you that we didn't mean to make our
mistakes look like a dance. All that big booty attitude in those small Bay Area jeans.

How many times have they told us that we are marred and marked by the failures
with which we thirst to atone?

Yes, we mourn, but let us celebrate too. We are Warriors.

Hello or goodbye? They extend reluctant salutations. And still, we let them into
our living room.

Oakland, they call you riotous, though you're just a mouth full of Pop Rocks.

To claim that your nightfall is endless is easy. If they knew how to read the darkness,
they would have figured it out by now:

the object that casts the biggest shadow is the one closest to the light.

U CAN'T TOUCH THIS
Oakland, CA, 1990

My 6th birthday gift
was a pair of Hammer pants
made of real kente.

LESSONS ON RHOTACIZING: A SHIBBOLETH

after Aracelis Girmay

da(r)k

It found my mouth when I was four. My father plucked the seed of sound from Pam Moore's afternoon news report.

He liked the way she pronounced the second consonant of her last name, how it bounced like a lottery Super Ball, from the screen into our living room. With closed eyes, there was no way to trace where it had been. This lithe, little melody was too correct to ever be asked to repeat itself until it disappeared.

gi(r)l

My mother washed the slippery letter, then planted it in the spongy soil of my mouth. It sprouted into a singular tendril, and grew to lap air from the ledge of my lip, then sift its way through my teeth.

They watched me like the news: my Californian accent curled the edges of my words like a patriotic breeze tickling the American flag at Oakland City Hall.

lea(r)ns

No one cared to know the weight of the anvil between my gums or the ache of the muscles in my jaw. Why a girl like me could sit in the front row of class. How a country died in my mouth, so I could reap a ghost.

The teachers rewarded the flight of my white girl music, how it carried no black note on its wings.

hu(r)t

I couldn't satisfy the playground checkpoint. The other brown girls blinked at me like all of the doors that would ever slam in their faces.

I learned to play double Dutch alone, with the spit and two-vine split of my tongue.

5

MOTHER'S RULES

for my mother, Agatha Kamara

I.   If you see me praying in the living room, never sit in front of me. You are not God.

II.   When we go to a restaurant and I don't know any foods on the menu, never order me a meal that is spelled with silent letters. I came to eat, not to explore.

III.   You didn't *make* food. No. God, did. You *cooked* food. Watch your English. Watch your faith.

IV.   Your Krio is offensive. When you speak, you sound like Shabba Ranks. Your accent is funny, but keep practicing. It is the only way we will be able to gossip in peace while at the supermarket.

V.   Try to learn the language of your lover and his family. They could be smiling to your face and getting ready to trade you for 6 goats and 3 mules during your first trip to their homeland.

VI.   If anyone stares at you for too long (more than 5 seconds), start speaking an imaginary language while maintaining eye contact. They will be the first to look away.

VII.   Consider the consequence of purchasing human hair wigs, secondhand clothing, and used furniture. Maybe you will feel beautiful, and also save money, but you never know whose bad luck or misfortune will be sitting on your head, body, or in the home in which you sleep. Buy what you can truly afford.

VIII.   Your father's Muslim, so you are too (1989–1993).
I am Christian, so you are too (1993–2012).
I am Catholic now, but you keep praying (2012–present).

IX.   You laugh at me now. Like I laughed at my mother. Like she laughed at hers. Like your daughters will laugh at you. And I will live long enough to forgive your folly.

X.   Just make sure to pray.

Amen.

BESAYDOO

While sipping coffee in my mother's Toyota, we hear the birdcall of two teenage
boys in the parking lot: *Aiight*, one says, *Besaydoo*, the other returns, as they reach
for each other. Their cupped handshake pops like the first fat firecrackers of summer,

their fingers shimmy as if they're solving a Rubik's cube just beyond our sight. Moments
later, their Schwinns head in opposite directions. My mother turns to me, revealing the
milky, John-Waters-mustache-thin foam on her upper lip, *Wetin dem bin say?*

Besaydoo? Nar English? she asks, tickled by this tangle of new language. *Alright.*
Be safe dude, I pull apart each syllable like string cheese for her. *Oh yah, dem nar real padi,*
she smiles, surprisingly broken by the tenderness expressed by what half my family might call

thugs. *Besaydoo. Besaydoo. Besaydoo,* we chirp in the car, then nightly into our phones
after I leave California. *Besaydoo,* she says as she softly muffles the rattling of my bones
in newfound sobriety. *Besaydoo,* I say years later, her response made raspy by an oxygen

treatment at the ER. *Besaydoo,* we whisper to each other across the country. Like
some word from deep in a somewhere too newborn-pure for the outdoors, but we
saw those two boys do it, in broad daylight, under a decadent, ruinous sun. *Besaydoo.*

Besaydoo, we say, *Besaydoo,* and split one more for the road. For all this struggle.
Tumble. Drown. Besaydoo, we say. To get on the good foot. We get off of the phone,
tight like the bulbous air of two palms that have just kissed.

A BRIEF BIOGRAPHY OF MY NAME

I. Djeli   Mende: blood.
                    Meaning, use the river in my vein
                    to paint a story that dries
                    the color of a bruise when meeting with air
                    and the passage of time.

Jelimuso   Female griot, a story pulsing in every blood cell.

                    Francis Cole, is a hotel porter who
                    is all obsidian and grin. On my last day in
                    Philadelphia, he tells me I am named after
                    a caste of West African storytellers.
                    He is a stranger who shares my mother's
                    maiden name, one that is not common
                    to where they are from.

Yalie,   I am made from the obsession of detail.

II. Sauda   Swahili: dark complexioned.

Fatat sawda   Arabic: Black girl.   فتاة سوداء

                    When my father tells me that I am named after
                    my reflection, I think he's lying.

Saweda,   Who would wait so long to tell their teenaged
                    daughter a story that might save their life?
                    If I'd known at thirteen that they'd place a nocturne
                    between my names, I wouldn't have wished to skin the night sky.
                    I wouldn't have sought the sound of whiteness
                    if I'd known that I was a song strained from indigo.
                    A note wrapped in lapis lazuli.

III. Kamara,   Bantu: teacher; one who learns from experience.

~~Masuba~~   In 1945 (maybe), my grandaunt lops off my last name like a hand that has
stolen. It is cut and left on the side of a red dirt road and disappears
under the tangerine heat of the Makorseh sun. As I write this,
my mother asks why the village name matters if no one in Oakland knows where
Makorseh is. Maybe she is talking about me.

Nobody dignifies this loss with memory. I make myth for peace.

Masuba   I: one who gathers, in order to understand the weight of the hole.

to Lumpia, your name itself sounds like a word
of praise, three syllables carving the mouth into
the shape of an eager bite.

O, savory, tubular fruit blooming in the hollow
of a hot pot of golden vegetable oil, where
does your labor end? Great unifier of tribes,

your taste has been known to tantalize the tongues
of our parents, fill their Limba, Fullah, Krio, Temne,
Mende, Susu, and Madingo mouths with enough

shredded cabbage and fried pork to convince them
that there was more to do at birthday parties and
funerals than bicker about political corruption.

You always came to the party on a silver tray, you and
your friends. Crisp and browned, each of you resting
atop the other in cheerleader pyramid formation.

O, Sierra Leonean eggroll, no one dared wasting you.
Never left you bitten next to a spoonful of jollof rice
drowning in the red paisley oil of its tomato stew.

You were always claimed, unlike the nameless, half-full Guinness
bottles abandoned on banquet tables by those dancing
too hard to Dr. Oloh to remember which drink was theirs.

Would you believe that I almost lost a friend because of you?
She told me that you'd been born on Cebu City's shore.
That all these years, you'd been a catered specialty.

I fired back, telling her that you called my name like family,
like our dipping sauce came from the same ocean.
I argued until I crumbled like the flakes that fell

from your sides and sank to the bottom of the deep fryer.

You are the friendliest outsider I've ever known.

When I squint my eyes, you still look like the color of my fingers.

How could you not be mine?

SPACE

At the age of 7, a letter was plucked from my name
as a test to see who would catch the error. To see

who'd care enough to go search for the rest of
me.

For about 4 months, my name appeared as *Yale*
on the page.

A part of me wonders why some names are sweeter than others
and become the nectar that pools at the base of our memory.

Would anyone let ssabelle, Rchard, Elzabeth,
or Snclar escape from the 9th letter of the alphabet?

Me and my broken name, less heavy than before,
began to float away to somewhere else.

No search party was sent to check between the
monkey bars, under the desks, my cubby,

or the palms of my hands. There was no red pen
to correct the flaw.

Nobody else played the game, so there's no
record of the joyful sound that was made when

the long-lost *me* found the small, brown, *I*.

EATING MALOMBO FRUIT IN FREETOWN, 1989

My Uncle Sonny cupped the malombo fruit in his palms. Between his ebony hands, it looked like a tired orange that had rolled on an unpaved dirt road for one thousand years. He must have noticed me trying to peel the fruit, which is the first mistake anyone makes when they have not eaten it before. He squeezed it until a little bit of it shot out of itself, like a pulpy lava bullet onto my grandmother's floor. I loosened a slippery knot of its tangy flesh and placed it in my mouth.

Malombo was the flavor before English—honeyed and tart, it slid across my tongue like a marble in a pinball machine. A stranger to fruit with pits, that which I could not chew, I pushed to the back of my throat.

The pit swam in my throat like a tourist. My uncle laughed at my puckered lips and bulging eyes—he told me not to worry. Told me that before I had the chance to die or become a giant malombo pit, it would pass eventually through me.

On an early morning phone call from Oakland, my sister still says that this is her story, that her throat was where the pit lodged itself and that Uncle Sonny had not laughed and grandmother's floor was the dirt outside. That it never happened to me, though I know it so well, the breathlessness of a thing being wedged in a place it does not belong.

We cannot agree; the moment must be hers or mine. When we asked our mother who this keepsake belonged to, she split the ghost fruit between us.

We tussle over a pit. We'd both rather choke than have no story at all.

DUTTYBOX

It happened almost always just months after each birth: the baby,
brown, thick, dimpled, alive with coo and gurgle, would breathe
no more. No medical examiner could explain why, and the mother
would commemorate the passing with clockwork lament:

a wail climbing up her throat hot and fierce as bile. Three times,
Mabinty Kanu lost her babies before they knew how to walk or say
their own name. Doera learned how to stand by holding a wall,
Mahfereh could crawl in circles, and Yebu knew only how to sit up

by the end of his first and last rainy season. Mabinty stopped rubbing
her belly after it arrived again, the feeling of dread dragging its wet,
heavy tongue over her womb. It tasted her love for her unborn, too sweetsop
sugary to not take a bite, so she began to strain the juice from her own voice.

Duttybox, she started to call the unborn, named him trash, gliding her fingers
along the watermelon print of her stretch marks. Named him something to bitter
the blessing, to sour the amniotic fluid in which he floated, to rot the umbilical cord,
to wrap him in filth, in refuse, in utero. It worked. Duttybox swam through

Mabinty's birth canal, a fake filthy so real, he was unwanted by the hand of the beyond.
How do you turn Death's stomach?

Love a child who is never quite pulled from the trenches of dirt.

RESURRECTION

Her mouth still cages mourning. The dry and bitten-tongue
hum between her teeth cuts through the baritone car engines
that climb the hills toward the city's flamingo-pink sunset.

My mother buries a serving of last night's krain-krain stew
and rice in between our garden's lemon tree and tomato bush.

She presses sienna hands over the soil to feed
my grandmother's spirit, then opens the bottle.
An amber stream of Meyer's rum soaks the soil below.
She prays for her mother to return in a knot of delight:

> Be silver Polaris dots dancing at the sides of my eyes,
> velvet whispers guiding breath, and honey smoothing
> over the tremulous voice of loss. Be the surprise air
> that dances through grief's gills.

In the forty days since she's passed, my mother, Aunt Margaret,
Uncle Samuel, and Uncle Harold only speak of her in present tense, as if
this persuades the earth to preserve her skin instead of consume it.

My grandmother's body rests in Freetown,
while they feed her memory in Oakland.

On the forty-first morning, we stand at the table around
my grandmother's dinner plate. A dent in the black-eyed
peas and a desert where water once filled her drinking glass.

She's accepted the invitation. My grandmother
returns in the wind. A small celebration begins.

My mother, aunt, and uncles dance and make melody for the
ghost of their mother. For her bite and gulp, her thirst and hunger.

I become a lyre bird mimicking their sound, unsure of what
grief means in the hyphen of my African and American throat.

I watch them bend time for my grandmother until she is alive.
They sift her light again and again through the prism of a final breath.

The dead only die when the living refuse to sing for them.

A HAIKU FOR THE BUS: 54 FRUITVALE BART STATION/MERRITT COLLEGE
Oakland, CA

She mouths psalms while the
other reads Sojourner Truth.
A bus. An altar.

GRAB BAG (MAY 1998)

After watching a grainy video of a million sperm swimming
upstream in pursuit of a singular egg, followed by a short film

imploring boys to wear loose jeans in order to preserve this
very count, we arrive at this week's highlight, and most

of the reason why I decide this will be the first and only time
I forge my mother's signature on a permission slip:

the magical sex grab bag. Ms. Smith instructs us to neatly write
our anonymous questions on small scrolls of paper to be placed

inside the plum crushed velvet pouch. The Life Science
classroom pulses with the sounds of quickly moving

No. 2 pencils and the backs of hands dusting eraser bits
from desks to floor. Old Spice and Juniper Breeze grip the air.

Amidst the squeak of uneven adolescent voices, Ms. Smith
smiles, shakes the sack, then loosens its drawstring, as if

to soon announce the winner of a sweepstake. One student
inquires: "Will having sex doggy style give you butt babies?"

Another asks, "Are there hecka ways to not be a virgin
no more?" Ms. Smith teaches us the word *cunnilingus*

and explains its meaning. "That's hella nasty," Milton tries
to mumble under his breath. "Are your findings based on your

being a cunnilingus connoisseur?" Ms. Smith retorts slickly with an
eyebrow raised in his direction. The overwhelm and foreignness

of these syllables reduces him to a sheepish grin, his butterscotch
face crumples to the form of a rare and quiet defeat.

I neither remember my question, nor
owning my body back then.

Ms. Smith constantly fans herself, and runs her hand over her
crystal ball belly. Under the fluorescent light, she glistens how

I imagine a freshly beached mermaid might. She'll be leaving us
in a few weeks to have her baby. She plucks the next question

quickly, then squints as if shooting lasers onto the squiggle
of words, shakes her head, and rolls her eyes.

She thinks someone in the class is playing.
"I'm not *even* going to answer this one."

Marshelle, who is sitting next to me, nervously chuckles
with a bit of her tongue peeking from between her gapped teeth.

"She read my question." She cups her hands onto my ears and whispers:
"How come niggas always tryna make you suck they dick?"

I snicker breathily so that she won't feel alone. Marshelle and I
are quiet for the rest of the class period.

Ms. Smith keeps talking, but I no longer hear her voice.
A disappointment rings in my ears. Sex ed is over for me.

Ms. Smith becomes what I attempted to escape—the deadbolt
lock over a girl's body. The untrained hand too rough for the tender

and growing. Two decades later, I wonder if Ms. Smith has learned
the texture of peril—how to use the thorns of language as a guide

to the center of its fruit, before disposing it in haste. I imagine
what variation of the question would have merited a response from

Ms. Smith: "How are boys learning to use their bodies like weapons, Ms. Smith?
Why doesn't he want to hear my voice, Ms. Smith?

Why doesn't he know the difference between a request and a demand, Ms. Smith?
When does the soreness subside after your heads been shoved into the center

of a boy's body, Ms. Smith? Can I say no, Ms. Smith? My name is Marshelle,
and I will be the first pregnant girl in your 8th grade Life Science class—

can you help me, Ms. Smith?" I needed Ms. Smith too for what she might not
be able to give—a voice to fight the fear of all the flowers sprouting within me,

words to battle any hands trying to uproot me before my season. That week
we thirsted for a grown woman whose water might help save our tiny lives.

SWEET BABY FABULIST

for my nephew, Elijah

In the third year of Elijah's life, black olives were Black.
And green olives were Black, too. Even the bubbling pot

of sunset-colored palm oil and plasas, was given the name Black
soup. He so adored Tolee, that he'd watch *Ni Hao, Kai-Lan* every

noon; Tolee was no longer a koala, but now his favorite Black
cartoon. Black was the boy Elijah,

and his finger tugging at heaven for fire. Black
were his dimpled knuckles when he pressed his hands to pray. Black

was the hue of the peace that he desired, the anointing oil he
rubbed on all that made him smile throughout the day. Black

is what he called the world, because he heard it from his Black
mother. Black is what he called the universe,

to show us how much he loved her. Black
were the rainbows, the full moon and the deep nightfall.

Black were the rivers and sky. God was as Black
as the autumn breeze's call. Black

was as crisp as the crust of sweet potato pie. Black
was a brilliant, pulsing light—too bright to be ignored. Black

sings the joyful chest from which all fears have been unmoored.
Black is the sight of a little boy finding his reflection in all things. Black

is what a little boy called us, so what else could we sing? If Black
is the chorus, an eternal echo of this one-word song,

then what is the color in the hollow of the mouth that would tell
him that what he is living is wrong?

I ASK MY BROTHER JONATHAN TO WRITE ABOUT OAKLAND, AND HE DESCRIBES HIS ROOM:

for D.R.

* *Night, The Wretched of the Earth*, and *This Is How You Lose Her* on his desk.
* The yellow legal pad with the line drawn down the center. Pros and cons of attending either Stanford or Columbia.
* Pearlescent sunlight pushing through the blinds and slicing stripes on bed and body.
* How tiny tomato sauce splotches and the remaining angel hair noodles look like Pollock's *Number 17, 1949* against the white lunch plate.
* The arm that tick-ticks around the silhouette of the Jumpman clock.

I wait for fire to burst once again between the hands of this chocolate wunderkind. For electricity to dance through the fingers of a young poet. Instead, Jonathan offers me an inventory of his possessions. And I wonder why he's chosen the words that do not breathe a kaleidoscopic fury into the cityscape's slate hue.

At the bottom of the message, he includes the parts of his body that he's most proud to own:

* Cinnamon hands. Straight teeth. An orange wedge smile. Peace between his left and right brain. A heart that isn't afraid of either side. A perfect canvas of skin.

Jonathan will not write about Mandana Boulevard, the six photos he took of the lady's garden before she called the police.

Jonathan imagines:
* Golden poppies sprouting between the novels on the bookshelf.
* Figs dropping from the tree attached to his door and rolling onto the cream-colored carpet.
* Wet fingertips caked with sugar for the hummingbirds flying out of his memory.
* A vine of thorns wrapping around the perimeter of the window frame so that they won't follow him home.
* The squad car driving past him, not using its siren to call his name.

He has no reason to leave his house if the most forgiving parts of the city are rendered in his dream.

Jonathan is creating a new town, where a young Black man lives in a garden. Where his body is unfettered by the terror of others' imagination: when he hugs his own flesh, the "X" his arms make across his chest is not mistaken for a target.

He finds himself too beautiful to not be in hiding.

MARSHAWN

Super Bowl XLIX Media Day, 2015

When you say "I'm only here, so I won't get fined," I feel my heart
boom-booming beneath the lapel of my corporate grey blazer.

I keep refreshing the YouTubed you in my office: with the *ka-tink* of
the mouse click, I see you, see me, see you, see us.

The questions keep cascading from the reporters' lips, their voices close,
but they themselves can't even catch their reflections off the onyx glint

of your stunna shades or the saffron gloss of your gold tooth. You
are in Beast Mode, yards ahead, running a play foreign to those

unencumbered by neither the weight of fatigue, nor public displays of
perfection. In crushing irony, The Verve's "Bittersweet Symphony" fills

the silences designated for your responses that never come. "I'm only here
so I won't get fined," you repeat into the microphones and recorders

hovering above the camera frame and podium, roving like a cluster of angry
clouds ready to storm all over the *I shall not be moved* of you, ready to storm

all over your navy blue and grey fitted cap that covers your crimped locs,
the licorice sticks that dust your shoulders every time

you turn your head toward another question with
the same answer: "   ."

In the span of 4 minutes and 51 seconds, you say it twenty-six more times
for the people in the back, behind the back, back to front, and back

to the future. By the 3rd video replay, I close my office door and send
this hallowed footage to my homegirls, like *Can you believe what he just did?*

Awestruck. Nonplussed. Gobsmacked. I am so grateful and jealous of
you: Marshawn,

I too have thought ten times about what I say and which one of my not-
so-many words will be melted down and fashioned into a spear destined

for the flesh covering my ribcage. I too have wanted to become a miracle
in my own Black mouth, say nothing when I've been urged to forecast

the future of any team I belong to or the failings of my own tongue or body.

I swivel in my desk chair and think about the long table at which
I will have to sit in less than hour, all of the ways I will be misread

and misheard, wishing I could paint the board room walls with your
seven-word protection prayer, but instead I forward the video

to those who need it—in classrooms, in cubicles, in courtrooms,
on sidewalks, in transit, far from home. We watch your art

immaculate—a still life of goofy questions. All of their inquiries
rise, then fall to the floor. What strange, discolored, plastic fruit you

do not eat. I keep your psalm under my tongue like a blade, then remember who
I am and tuck it between my two front teeth. I smile when I tire of the game.

My silence, a nice-nasty so smooth, it honeys, then butters, the air.

REKIA AND OSCAR AND ALL OF THEIR SKY COUSINS

According to bird-watchers, sparrows are also known
as little brown jobs, because of how difficult it is

to identify them by species. It seems that for once,

a mass of brown bodies living in resounding
similarity will be the very thing that saves them.

Watch them fly with a preternatural ease—
as if they were born in the afterlife.

They glide slowly as they approach evening,
unaware that their kind is not meant to travel

alone, under the blueberry gauze of nightfall.

Sparrows are social birds: they make a rest stop
of the stretch of sky that separates this world

from the next. See strangers become kin:

a thousand birds chirp into each other's
drying bullet wounds.

Sparrows enjoy group singing.

Which is to say that their sound is
a chorus soaked in molasses.

Which is a gospel.

Touching wing to wing, they constellate,
and keep the world ablaze.

Sparrows become sky cousins.

Family is derived from the word famulus,
which is a servant, oftentimes to a magician.

A star is defined as a luminous piece of plasma held
together by its own gravity. Which is a form of magic.

And to make melody from grief is a way
to serve each other's heart.

But a dirge is heavy.

They are too tired to ponder the strength
of their own bodies.

Instead, they sing like this isn't death.

LE CHAMP LEXICAL #1: L'ESPOIR (EN 2020 C'EST)

after AM

Comme le mode de vie. Comme la discipline. Comme la rigueur.

Comme la renaissance. Comme la purge.   Comme le radicalisme.

Come realism.   Comme la subversion.   Comme le défi.

Come defeat.   Comme l'hymne.   *Come   limb.*

Comme la fortitude. Comme le travail.   *Come try.*

Comme le rythme.   *Come boom.*   *Come bip.*

Come cha-ching.   Comme l'investissement.   Comme le dividende.

Comme la monnaie. Comme le dépôt.   Comme le retrait.

Come reclaim. Comme la réclamation.   Comme le langage.

Comme le verbe. *Come verve.* Comme le nom. Comme le mot.

Come, oh. Comme l'eau.   Comme la boisson.

Come, fam. Comme la faim. Comme la nourriture.

Comme la passion.   *Come pass on.*   *Come rest.*

Comme la respiration.   *Come breath.*

Come breathe.   *Come speak.*   *Come call.*

Comme la réponse.   *Come to.*   *Come one.*

Comme le son.   Comme la sonnerie.   *Come bomb.*

Come silence.   Comme le baume.   Comme le psaume.

Come poem.
Come home.

Comme hier.   *Come year.*   Comme l'infini. *Come beyond.*
Comme oui.

Comme oui.

Comme oui.   *We come.*

that in the early '80s, Aunty X moved to New Jersey, though I'm not sure where she lived. (Perth Amboy? Newark? Orange?) At some point, she worked in a hospital, probably fluffing the stiff pillows of elders or even using a bare thumb to lift dribble from a thin lip. The old folks loved her—the first African they'd ever met. *Weird British spelling. Pretty good English, though.* Charming in an American adjacent way.

By her own admission, she was too cute for her own good. Aunty X was all mahogany, a head full of dripless Jheri curls, staccato laughter, small waist, and a bad winking habit. Her hip action? Like a slow motion metronome whenever Bunny Mack was on rotation at the disco. She was a threat to too many married men. Which is why some nervous and evil wife made the call. So, they showed up at her job. Them. The ones with the official badges, the clipboards, the multicolor click Bic pens, and the questions about her paper and her papers.

On what floor can we find her? the agents ask, unaware of the morning elevator's mixed company. *The 5th* Aunty X's manager lies, while stepping on her shoe like a gas pedal on the expressway. Aunty X gets it, and folds into her own breath like a ghost. *Excuse us*, they say, unknowingly brushing past her in their exit. Aunty X goes up to the 8th floor. A nurse's assistant whisks her to the 9th. With a blanket in hand, she leaves the America she knows.

While they comb the building, she hides in the morgue. Shift nurses come and leave offerings in this tundra of shelved cadavers. Black tea. Inspect. Turkey sandwich. Inspect. Apple sauce. Inspect. Aunty X's teeth chatter. Inspect. *Are you okay?* Inspect. Blanket. Inspect. Wait. Inspect. Wait. Inspect. She looks at her watch—the cold metal on her wrist made colder by the absence of time in this new country.

Eventually, they leave. Aunty X inhales and thaws out in a staff room. They halfway promise to return, though they never do. The hospital keeps her and gives her more hours, perhaps impressed by how well she plays dead. She blesses them still.

Aunty X tells me this in a hotel room on a cool September evening. The air conditioner blasts against her bare shoulders. She hands me a $100 bill. *Get some boots*, she says. *This winter will be cold.*

SOUVENIR

University of West Indies, Cave Hill, Barbados

Come, do this, Ms. Margaret calls out to me. And so
        I leave her air-conditioned office, then follow.
We stand here under the hot fist of this Bajan sky. Each
        of our right arms is extended. She rotates
her wrist, then I swivel mine. Our bracelets clang
        against the wind, against
the Shak Shak tree's gentle drumming,
        against the barren parking lot's cratered
face upon which we plant our feet.
        We begin to melt from woman to solid to liquid.

From the main office window, it must look
        like we are dancing, though if our shadows
told the story, it would say that our limbs
        are trying to twist the world like a wind-up
toy. She points to the first sweat beads
        that congregate at the shore of my forearm
like a handful of cabochons. They burst into
        prismatic rivulets. Ms. Margaret watches
my summer flesh alchemize. She is wide
        grinned as I learn the secret: how in this season,
we become black opal under each other's watchful eye.
        A week later, I smuggle myself through customs.

In America, I try it again and again: the magic
        trick in which I make a rainbow of my skin
every time it storms in this nation that I call home.

PEST CONTROL

The long mot arata is a type of Sierra Leonean rodent that strikes its prey in sleep. It nibbles away at its victims while they are nestled in deep repose. Its teeth sand down callouses until they reveal scarlet and beige flesh.

Though its stomach collapses under the anvil of hunger, this mouse has principle. It takes tiny breaks to purse its lips and push a stream of cold wind onto its target's feet, so as to offset any irritation that may tussle the unsuspecting out of slumber.

Though I don't know if anyone in my family could positively identify
the *long mot arata* in a lineup of offenders, their certitude of the mouse's
existence is irrefutable; it lies in the way they express the betrayal
they have often felt at daybreak:

They are disturbed by the scene:
short brown hairs flecked on the bed
and maroon paw prints inked
by their own blood.

Not even the simple act of rest comes without profound suffering.

For most of my life, I have been haunted by the *long mot arata*, and
taught to question the motives of friends just like these creatures,
to doubt the admiration of anyone who loves me without good
enough reason,

to look for punctured heels following any
explosion of praise leaving a familiar mouth.

I had fallen many times from this spell:

the cool current passing over my toes
before seeing a bit of myself hanging
from your smiling lips.

At times, I feel sorry for myself. The constant expectation of
wounds, anticipating your breath to coat my heels with ice
before you try to take my feet and walk away from me. This,
too, creates its own death: living to catch a pest.

Not even the simple act of rest comes without profound suffering.

> I have gathered all of your forgotten
> fur from my nightstand drawer and
> plastered it to my body.

> The moon makes an indigo silhouette
> of your whiskers and snout.

> Still and quiet, I wonder just when
> you will notice how long you have been
> eating yourself in the dark.

A HAIKU FOR THE TRAIN: LIGNE 7/ CORNEUVE-VILLEJUIF

Paris, France

A man counting crack
rocks gives up his seat for two
girls and their father.

SOUMISSION CHIMIQUE

Paris, France

I must have looked too pathetic to jack. Like the kind of woman that
even a thief has mercy for, simply because it appears that so much

has already been taken from her.

In the half of the metro ride that I remember, I see a sliver of
my brown body between the slow-motion flutter of heavy eyelids.

The train jerks back & forth until what used to
be beer in my stomach froths into an

unexpected sleep. I fade to ghost.

Every speculation of what happened on that particular evening in Paris
between the hours of 8:30 p.m. & dusk passes like exhaust over

my face.

Maybe he boarded the metro with me at Châtelet, followed me home to
Pantin, tapping his feet lightly on the snow behind me, but was too slow to

squeeze

into the complex. I must have locked the apartment gate so quickly
that the door's slam sounded more final than my clumsy fingers could

actually muster.

Or did he get off the train before me—my metro ride too long for his
liking: twenty-five minutes, when he only had fifteen to

get the job done.

Or maybe he never left the bar, never moved from behind the counter &
got hard

just seeing me begin to crumple

on my stool only a quarter into my first & only Maredsous ale.

He might have handed me the drink while smiling at me, tickled by the
quiet power of his finger, a dirty wand plunging into the hollow

of my thistle glass.

I'll never know exactly where the story starts. In which sip the sedative
activated, when its hushed shrapnel exploded against

every soft pink wall of me.

That night I went home and made an omelet. Burnt it till the apartment
smoked up like the gates of hell.

Stumbled

to bed with my party clothes on, and at 10:30, I was still confusing the
collapse of my limbs as a weakness that was entirely my fault.

With every two hours that passed, I kept snapping the branches of sleep.
Heard the winter wind hiss through the shutters.

Felt a fire around my pillow.

That night, I learned that danger had a heat. Passed closely to the face, buzzed &
snarled and took a couple of steps back, just to look at me in the eyes before

it did what it wanted.

But couldn't.

I must have locked the apartment gate so quickly that the door's
slam sounded more final than my clumsy fingers could

actually muster.

The next morning, I found my apartment key still in the door stuck stiff & deep,

like a dagger in flesh.

What hand guided me through an evening of one thousand
almost deaths?

What bell clanged in my sternum like a call to the town square of my spirit?

From the indigo of that evening until the seagull grey of the
sky the morning after,

I sat up & lied down.
And sat up & lied down.
Like a drill. Like a torture.
Like a ritual. Like I knew how to break a spell.
Like something was being kneaded out of me.
Like I needed something to be out of me.

Like I already hated what would await me in the
back of my head & behind my eyes

if I let myself go.

Like even five years later & in America,
I'm still not snapping in & out of sleep,
searching for a word in any language to

define this stubborn pulse—

What do we call the woman that survives poison?

When she is returned to her memory,
And she is given back to her breath,
And she emerges from the silence of her
vanishing—

Call me a woman who is just now learning
how to accept how close
I was to falling into darkness.

Call me someone's failed project: a sharp light
on evil.

Call me the flicker of sun between heavy
eyelids.

Call me daybreak.

I believe there's no excuse for us not to be feared or [not to be] protected in our sleep. See in our sleep, we're our most vulnerable. With our eyes closed, we are in dreamland . . . people could break in your house, steal all your goods, they could come kill you, they could shoot you. They could do ALL these things! So what do you do (this is an education for y'all in this building)? You set your phone on audio . . . biblical audio. You set it by your pillow so that you're prayed up. You're praying all the time so the word of God is above your head and beneath your feet . . . just all in yo' room. So if a muthaf*cka came in the room . . . YOU went out with God. If that bible is constantly going, I'm being fed in my sleep. I'm being protected.

And if you come in there, you're going to feel like two cents asking for change. Cause if you do something, you already know. God was in this room. (Angie Stone)

Ms. Angie, do you sleep with Mahalia Jackson's nectar pouring from your pillow?

> *Bless these walls / So firm and stout*
> *Keeping want / And trouble out*

Does her voice spill onto your sheets and soak you through to glowing, wet amber?

Each time you twitch in the crook of slumber, do you splatter stars onto the chalkboard-black walls of your bedroom?

Do you think this sight would be enough to scare away a thief?

Would it make a grown man think twice about inching toward the foot of your bed?

Could a psalm orbing from the iPhone speaker be its own type of ghost?

Could that convince an intruder to give up his own ghost?

Do you fear what you can't see when you are closed eyes?

Do you rest, anyway, surrendering to the dawn and dusk of your breath?

Do a watch of nightingales perch atop your limbs and wash their wings with the Carolina breeze of your pursed lips?

Do they chirrup loudly, like the underside of their song is a warning?

Do they croon like they are guarding your blood fruit?

Do you sing in return into the cosmos of God's rounded mouth?

Ms. Angie, is that the entrance of a dream? Of a dream? Of a dream?

Is a dream permission to swim naked through the iridescent tunnel of your hard-earned sleep?

Do you become more hallowed and holographic as midnight burrows into its azurite malachite, self?

Ms. Angie, are you the galaxy?

BLOOMINGTON, INDIANA PART I

Before I learn to die unto myself, I am told, by a pastor who I had just met, when visiting an aunt who I had only previously spoken to on the phone, that my life could kill me. The way I hold myself, he says, between the pinch of the index finger and thumb, is simply not enough. I tussle with the warning, then let it ring in the middle of my ear for a week before I begin to empty myself of myself. I'd never been told this by a stranger, but think I agree. I believe I could be slowly dying, particularly when thinking of every morning after every evening that started out as an escape.

I say farewell to the comforts of Indiana that make the move from the Bay Area *feel* easy. These comforts are so cheap that they appear exotic—Goodbye, $3 shots and $2 pints. I exhale the last American Spirit and clean the final Bulleit wound. I let go of my acquaintance with bile; I upchuck the garnet and bubble gut the amber of Midwestern excess. I think being around friends who still partake in a life that is not good for me will have no effect, but in their presence, I feel the urge to backstep. A strange, loud-booming, heart-racing anxiety gnaws at me from the inside. This ugly sensation is the beginning of a lifestyle change.

I erase Tinder, but before I do, I stare long at the handsome man who pins down an antlered creature in his profile pic. In real life, I scrub all the John Deere from the pore and the membrane and the bedsheet. There is so much on which to swipe left in my own life.

This business of being careful is heavy. I commit tentatively. I stay away from bars as often as I can, which means missing out on some MFA events. I skip parties, too. Though I stop drinking, I leave a bottle of Cardinal vodka in my fridge for a month before throwing it out. Though I become celibate, I don't erase the numbers of my favorites. Nothing is completely immediate. There is an ever-so-slight feeling of safety in the thought of returning to the ritual of toxic behavior.

I don't quite know what is possible in my own life, though I want to be a writer and wish to be more centered. The difficulty here is I don't understand the extent of wishing and hoping, or the far reaches of dreaming. I keep being told that permanent change cannot be made in private. I don't understand that fully either, but want to hear from others.

For the first time in my life, I begin to go to church, but not before saying *no* to many: the church where the music sounds distorted; the one where the pastor-in-training lays hands on my head to perform a holiness I cannot feel; the one with the delicious Communion bread and banjoes, but is far too quiet for my West African sensibilities. I join a Baptist church where they shout and cry, where

40

everyone is broken, but trying. The one in which honest sinners are happy to hold my hand and double squeeze my knuckle at the end of prayer. Mercy.

I like that the church is walking distance from my home, but feel worried about attacks on Black congregations. One of the parishioners is a sheriff. He makes sure to always park his squad car in front of the church. He prays and sings mellifluously throughout every service. My stomach knots after the first time I see it; when he turns to put tithes in the collection plate, the motion reveals his holstered gun. This is an open carry state, even in the sanctuary.

Community helps. Time helps, too. But really, solitude deserves more credit in the conversation on healing.

I become more able to steer clear of my ennui and my ratchet. I go to the library to study line breaks by myself. I tell my friends it's about to get weird, then lose most of them. Glory!

I find my favorite places to hide; one of them is in my kitchen. Something about the space gets me. It is small and tucked away. Like my life here. While it is a place to cook, it also a place to cry. To arc. To bend. To break. To come back together with no human watching.

I soothe with the book of John. Psalms. Pamplemousse La Croix. Vegan apple cider donuts. New wigs. Podcasts. My mouth, ever agape. Agape. Embouchure. After a season, I aqueous unravel in the waters of Baptism. After I dry, wet stained glass is still trickling from my ear. I find a metaphor in this, something about praise being messy. Most things are bright and the sound is loud. This is a type of rising from sleep.

All of this, in Bloomington, Indiana.

What I knew, but did not want to know, was that a friend was called a monkey and spat on around the corner from my apartment. What I remembered, but did not want to remember, was the car with the tinted windows that once followed me for blocks. What I recall, but want to forget, is why we never stop for gas in Martinsville. What doesn't surprise me is that neo-Nazis sell fresh produce at the farmers market.

I am certain the blood never dries in Indiana. I am also certain that the blood never loses its power.

This is where I found my God, nodding me awake.

Talitha koum. Talitha koum.

ELEGY FOR MY TWO STEP

Before the spirits left me, I used to sway with some sort of lubricated ease inside a dingy crescent of bodies that reeked of $2 Dickel shots and buzzed with Tinder pheromones.

I've become too slow for the radio tunes that once made me drop it on an Indiana dancefloor with strangers that never seemed to respect the full moon of a cypher.

This year, I watch the clock and my feet. Under the light of my dining room, there is no shadow to hide my disfigured shimmy.

Yes, I know I am out of place. These days, I am made of the looseness of the liquid I run away from—a fluid mess— my knees groove in one direction, while my ankles move in the other.

I am so soft and rhythmless, it's made some of my old friends mad enough to leave me.

Still, I rock content and offbeat like the naked ice cubes stacked in my red cup.

Yes, peace can look clumsy—I am often a matchstick unable to light

against the aggressive humping of humid strangers.

I sip-swallow the elixir of my brand-new sober spit, while my two heels beg for a more merciful gravity.

I dance an ugly dance, but my God it is an honest one.

There was a season of my girlhood, that I snapped so joyfully, that I bruised my middle finger. I hunger for the plum color of my birthright to return.

And so I stay indoors. And then I try again.

In my apartment, there is no dining table where one should be: I use the wood panel finish of the vacant floor as my greatest teacher.

I follow the compass needle tick of my own hips to trace how I got over. Such solitary work.

This body and its pewter silhouette against the patient white wall. A hand reaches out—

I touch my blessed, undying self.

METAPHORS FOR MY TWO STEP:

• name tag • resume •

• cover letter • elevator pitch •

• mission statement • not-for-profit •

• dot-org • best practices •

• hip autograph • ankle editing •

• toe kisses • shin signatures •

• foot cursive • nickname •

• white flag • surrender •

• province • territory •

• border • flag •

• mother tongue • root •

• family tree • coat of arms •

• broken branch • small dance •

• shy-girl glide • introvert bounce •

• perfume footed shimmy • Jesus walk •

• Rappers Delight • tonic water •
○ with lime!

• radio edit • kid-friendly •

• birth control • curfew •

• closed eyes • heaven somewhere •

• becoming Dorothy • ruby shoes •

• heel click • heel click •

• I wish I were home •

• I wish I were home •

• I wish • I wish •

• I wish • Good night •

A GOLDEN SHOVEL FOR MY FRIEND MICHAEL CHAN

This evening, I looked up a handful of synonyms for the word *incurable*.
What I think I may have found was either a small prayer in my thesaurus or

the rough draft of a steadfast psalm—the undoing of bad news. So
let me tell you about the words *eternal* and *undying*. And how they

are incandescent twins flitting through the bowels of what the diagnosis might say.
They are like the light between your teeth, Michael. Your sweet mouth, no

different from the sun, a mango pulp pulsing softly on U Street in the summer. My regrets
for sharing a simile about the country that lives above your tongue so late. No

excuse here, other than fearing a premature praise song would be a surrender to sadness.
A decade ago you showed me an onyx tattoo scrolled on your wrist. Though I no

longer recall the phrase on your skin, you smiled and warned me to not live a nothing
life, the type in which we become too boring to dream in the color of bling and we're

merely echoes of our own desires. Gardens afraid of water. You asked—*if we're not using all
of our fingers to cradle the blossom of this breath, then what are we really doing here?*

This is a new skill for me. To find wonder and not expectation in the gift of going on and on,
but haven't you been whispering this to me for years now, love? To massage and unearth

this stubborn thank you from my own chest? And now it is dusk and I open my shades to
a morning sky made of fig skin & fire. Can I call this magic *you*? Teach the universe to learn

the melody that ripens night into daybreak? I think it already knows. I hear it in the chirp and
peck of confident creatures, greeting the new day's fight & the chaos it promises to make.

I think we can make shields out of almost anything. For me, they are two eyes shut so good
and tight that my daydream becomes a prayer. And no nightmare leaves bruises on impact.

Is this the same for you? Do you hold yourself so close that you forget your armor is on?
Or do you feel my palms cradling your heart, fingers interlaced into the space of the other's.

A MOUTHFUL

Graeter's Ice Cream, Cincinnati, Ohio

A little girl of three or four struts to her seat
at an   ice cream parlor table.
Her mother,   two paces
behind,   orders   two scoops at the counter.
I study the danger bloom as
                                    her tiny body   rocks,
then   tip-tips
on one leg of the chair,   until the minute
melts and seconds of
                                    balance   vanish &
then the scream of the child.   Its roar digs into
us like a   hardworking
school bell,   its ring enough to kill
half of the would-have-been
bang and scrape of the   metal chair
against linoleum. I watch the girl too
shaken   to realize   she never hit the floor.
The mother crouches to her level.
Some of us are lucky   to learn that somewhere
between terror and healing   is language,
bone, and the mother's   question, a first
lesson in triage: Baby girl,
are you scared   or   are you hurt?

LISTENING TO NINA SIMONE SING "JUST LIKE TOM THUMB'S BLUES"
for DT

Under the comfort of   Cincinnati fog,
            I listen to your   voice:
                  a twirl   of
cocoa nib   and bergamot; an   acre
of semisweet   tenor notes   softly
pushing through   dimpled   loam;
an   onshore wind that cuts
through an Atlantic Ocean   wave.

How you   rub chalk maple   over
the head of   a screech   and   even
make a sweet thing of   the acrid.

While you did not draw   the map
that shows   the sticky trail
of Tom's   lugubriousness,
                  you fashioned
the compass that leads   to
the creaky side door of that   hostel
in   which he stayed   during
his Easter   sojourn in Juarez.

You, Aunty Nina,   are an ever ready
synonym for Polaris. Meta-raconteuse,
you dive into the marrow
                        of the marrow
of a story.
                  Now that is deep.

I think   I understand it now: Aunty
Nina, you sing each   woman
into a symbol
of some sort of ascension.

There's Melinda,   the holder of gloom,
who walks up   the forever
        of a wooden
                    staircase.
She waits for   the moment
to bear the obsidian   walls
of her mouth and her   honey-lined
gums to any hungry fool   that treks
behind her.

And then, there's St. Annie, who   is 1.
the patron saint of   miners   in the
        middle earth who sweatily lament
their subterranean homesick blues,   2.
the protectress of   capsized boats and
storms,   and 3.
the   hand resting on the boat
of a woman pushing the head of a storm
through her own middle earth.

Aunty Nina, aren't these   all metaphors
for reaching skyward?

And wouldn't you say that
                    this is your work?

I slow-scratch the   record   just
to hear the way you stretch   the word
ghost into 6   syllables.

And now there is a hole   on the speaker's
mesh that takes the shape of a hexagonal
set of   hips. A spirit   pushes
its way   through the busted geometry   of
the record   player.

You: floating, floating, up to the North Star.

THURIBLE

"I'll be loving you . . . until the day you are me and I am you."—Stevie Wonder

I know that homesickness is born from distance
and that distance cures home sickness.

And that rage is a big calcified hut of a heart
with one door, two rooms and a half-opened

window. And that you both sleep on
its floor when words are two mouths

full of broken teeth. And that this is a lineage thing.
From mother to daughter. I know that you will awaken

for two reasons: the whistle pitch of a ready kettle
on the stove or the fragrance of braided flowers swaying

at the lip of the open window. Today in Indiana,
I felt heat rising from my pulse points.

I spritzed both of your birthday present perfumes
onto my body as if they would never run out.

Lovely. I rubbed them into my wrists until my bracelets
clanged like laughter. *J'adore.*

Until I was joyful and almost bare boned. Until I saw
the human smoke of my good work.

Until my arms were incense. Until your gifts lifted
from my skin and glided on winter air, returning to you.

Until you dreamt until you couldn't. And you both
arrive in the kitchen and drink hot water.

And talk about the familiar scent of kin set aflame.

A POEM FOR MY UNCLE

After Nicole Sealey

My sister and mother say they saw my Uncle Solomon rise
from his own coffin at his funeral—say that with each pace,

his shadow disrobed from itself, until he appeared a stibnite
shimmer. My uncle came back from the dead the color of

a strobe light, float-walked above
the church's maroon carpet, pressing

into the pulse of every living thing in the sanctuary: into the glottal
howl of his ex-wife, then the dewy cheekbones of his estranged

sons, who too had that sweet potato-hued skin. I felt him too
that day, his voice, a silver dust, as fine as the

static between home videos of him cradling my tired infant body—

his voice, a small sliver of God urging me to stop
lip-synching the hymn,

While on others, thou art calling, he sings—do not pass me by . . .
While on others, thou art calling, he sings—do not pass me by . . .

lip-synching the hymn,
his voice, a small sliver of God urging me to stop

static between home videos of him cradling my tired infant body—

that day, his voice, a silver dust, as fine as the
sons, who too had that sweet potato-hued skin. I felt him too

howl of his ex-wife, then the dewy cheekbones of his estranged
into the pulse of every living thing in the sanctuary: into the glottal

the church's maroon carpet, pressing
a strobe light, float-walked above

shimmer. My uncle came back from the dead the color of
his shadow disrobed from itself, until he appeared a stibnite

from his own coffin at his funeral—say that with each pace,
My sister and mother say they saw my Uncle Solomon rise

Uncle, are we the sound of tongues turning to stained glass?

THREE DAYS BEFORE MY BAPTISM

For the past week, the knot housed in my womb
has thrashed against the inner wall of my stomach.

It is an always feeling. An anger spasms in my uterus
while I lie in bed. With every step that I take on my way

to wherever it is that I am walking, it juts out below my
belly button. I rub my middle in circles as if it finds the

back of an intruder who wants to hurt me, but thinks I may
first owe it love. But hadn't this been my whole life?

I'd spent so much time caring for the things that burned
me in the places I didn't know how to soothe.

Or how to reach. Three days before my baptism, I find the
words to whisper a sacred goodbye. I shower, sloughing

off dead skin mixed with lavender soap from my tired body.

It leaves me, a spongy burgundy corpse that looks like velvet
cloth passing between my legs. It looks back at me, blinded

by the shower's steam. I push it down with my toes through
the drain. I step on the face of a nightmare that is smaller

than my body, but bigger than time. Passed down from
shadowed hand to shadowed hand, imperceptible in the

charcoal bowels of my dreams, this is an ancient pain.

So old it has no name, so stubborn it traveled a century
to take hostage of my becoming. But my prayer is a furnace.

A flame runs down the back of a generational horror.
It loosens itself from my womb.

As I stomp, it scatters and runs toward the water.

REPAST IN THE DIVERSITY CENTER

We line up with our paper plates in hand: two pieces of white bread, packs
of mayo, mustard, and ketchup. There are tongs to grab the fixings: water runs

down the spine of the washed lettuce; it arches like a back snapping
out of a nightmare. Sliced tomatoes bleed into the foil pan holding them.

The Spicy Nacho Doritos rubs against the pink ripple of meat peeking
from between the bread slices. After every two or three deaths,

we are invited to grieve-eat ham sandwiches. I sit at a round table
and struggle to open my bag of chips between each microphoned voice

that laments another loss. How we've come together once more to eat
all that we cannot bury.

A man holds the mic like an ice cream cone:
I mean, I guess I'd be willing to die if I had to.

He tugs at the bottom of his untucked purple polo shirt.
I thought the food would taste better.

When I am sad, the noises in my head are louder. In my mouth,
the chips sound like someone walking on loose gravel. My people

need to *crunch* up. It's *crunch* or never. I'd rather *crunch* on my feet
than live on my knees. It seems I might miss the revolution eating

state-sponsored food. A white woman from the campus mental health clinic
offers counseling services. She stutters, then fades into the wall as if to make

space for Marvin as he croons his famed question into the speakers.
I'll tell you what's going on: the lemonade is too sweet for such an occasion.

I'd rather drink water. Cheesy stardust bruises the tips of my fingers.
It smears onto any surface I touch. I am marked. Lord, people are dying

and the only evidence of my mourning are these party hands.
What a bright color against these deep black blues.

I have to be honest: I only came because I was hungry.

HAIKU LOVE LETTERS FOR GABBY DOUGLAS

Nappy wins the gold.
        Medals hang from 4C curls.
                Your head holds glory.

They said *focus on*
        your edges. They must have meant
                both ends of the vault.

The *problem* is you
        love yourself whole. This is the
                most dangerous act.

                                      Bend, but do not break.
                        Your backflip: a metaphor
                                for this whole, Black, life.

If you'd placed your hand
        on your chest, then we wouldn't
                have heard your music.

Gabby, come knock on
        our doors. Ask us what we've named
                our dolls and daughters.

While mothers pray for
      your flight, babies watch your wings
           caress gym skyline.

                    We hold you close. Smile
                        when we touch the forests that
                            grow on our own heads.

VISITING NIA WILSON'S MEMORIAL SITE
Oakland, CA, July, 2018

I've forgotten how to dress for Oakland summers, ten toes exposed to a morning not yet ready to burn into something more   amber.
I cinch my hoodie   around my neck, trying to make heat that never comes to this body.

          It is a hard thing, to stare at the thing right in front of you.

So for now, I turn sideways and take field notes on mourners: a commuter says a short, neat prayer in front of the Macarthur BART
Station entrance, while another slowly scans the onyx sharpie ink tattooed over every concrete surface:

Too perfect   for the imperfect world. RIP. #Justice4Nia. Say her name. Sing her name.

                    I see you black girl.

A cursive wind ribbons through the tiny, golden flames at our feet. A passing stranger asks: *You know who keeps the candles lit?*

One empty fifth of Courvoisier gazes up at a wall holding one taped bouquet of flowers that looks down at two *You Are Worthy of Healing*
pamphlets below. Feet away, I spy the confetti of one gutted Philly cigar that   has made space   for the soul of   some   future or
past blunt.   Five stages of grief, I count, in total. *You know who keeps the candles lit?*

Black lives, the words read. *Black lives,* I think. Yes. *Black lives,* I think. Maybe? I read until a noun becomes a verb becomes as uncertain   as
my own skin.   O vigil. O archive of anti-death. O attempt at life.

                    O vigil. O archive of anti-death. O attempt at life.

O Nia,

you know who keeps the candles lit.

HOW TO WRITE AN EKPHRASTIC POEM ABOUT A NIA WILSON MEMORIAL PORTRAIT

Resist the temptation of making allusions to Nia becoming a heavenly ornament—
engage first with her life before rushing to canonization. Note what your query unearths:
Nia's graduation colors were green and gold—in a photo of the front rows of Dewey
Academy's commencement ceremony, a folding chair holds the almost sum total of

Nia's big day:
white roses; photos of her face and iconic, flawless, eyebrows; a cap and starched gown;
a graduation medal; and a high school diploma—fix your eyes on the photos again,
as one of them will eventually become the subject of a tribute that will become
the center of your work—

in it, honey-brown Nia squats and clasps her hands in a way that always makes girls
from Oakland look fierce—she dons a striped shirt that reminds you of the flavors of
Now and Later candies, and at the knees, her mid wash jeans are embellished with silver
ball gown sequins—

she rocks a pair of checkered Vans slip-on shoes, and her bamboo
earrings shine brassy and seem to be mid sway in the image—and speaking of earrings,
you return to her head, behind which the artist renders a halo whose color is hard to
describe—slightly separately, you recall a photo of Nia's pallbearers: a squad of Black
women decked out in ivory.

Tell your little sister to stop napping on the train after her work shift—

steady your eye on the halo behind Nia's head. Run its color across your tongue to find
its name: maybe it's the color of butterscotch button candy wrappers or the color of
the slick, sliced peaches in the Del Monte fruit cups—

run the halo's color across your fingers: move your eye from the crown of roses
and their leaves, and think of her resemblance to a Coptic saint, how she
seems to look beyond the day, her gaze affixed on a gate you cannot enter—start there.

Consider the implications of hovering so close to Black Death. What is the intention
behind the details you choose to curate? Think for an hour, a week, a season, a year—
then risk being wrong.

MEMORIALIZING NIA WILSON: 100 BLESSINGS

1.   Bless your 18 years.
2.   Bless the 19th, if even spent from an Oakland in the hereafter.
3.   Bless an unnamed eternity.
4.   Bless the stibnite hue of flight. My good God:
5.   Bless the ánima, and everything in and around the body.
6.   Bless the mandible; the deep ecru of bone; the 32 teeth.
7.   Bless the sepia organ: the skin.
8.   Bless the soft parts: the cheek; the neck; the mouth; the tongue; the voice.
9.   Bless the vessel.
10.   Bless your origin story: the magenta hollow of your mother's womb and the chestnut tint of your father's hand.
11.   Bless the site of desecration: 37.8291° N, 122.2670° W.
12.   Bless you whole again. Bless Oakland great again.
13.   Bless Blackness magnificent again.
14.   Bless the overlooked . . . the phenotype undamned.
15.   Bless technology and its digital griots.
16.   Bless collective memory; the hashtag; the electronic archive; the way it chronicles some sort of you.
17.   Bless your unfinished business—your dream of being an EMT— how the vocation's irony pushes against your death.
18.   Bless too, the joy: your Town Bizness style.
19.   Bless all the time it took you to get dressed for even a trip to the corner store.
20.   Bless the annoying things we do that create the fullness of our legacy.
21.   Bless the crown that holds the baby hairs.
22.   Bless the nimble toothbrush and the firm grip.
23.   Bless the cloud-thick gel.
24.   Bless the faithful, bangled wrist.
25.   Bless the cinematic motion of swirls on your edges.
26.   Bless the waves cascading off the cliffs of your temples.
27.   Bless your art everlasting.
28.   Bless you unshook as obsidian.
29.   Bless you unshook as onyx.
30.   Bless the scripture of your name.
31.   Bless the regal thread stitched into each letter of who you are and what you have been called into.
32.   Bless Nia, meaning *purpose*, or *intention*.
33.   Bless Wilson, meaning *son of will*, *fate*, or *destiny*.

34. Bless you whole again: Nia Daney Wilson.
35. Bless the circuitous path of hemoglobin.
36. Bless the blood and its peripatetic flow.
37. Bless your 5 brothers and 2 sisters.
38. Bless Tifa, who, struck by blade too, held you in her arms.
39. Bless her words: *I got you baby, I got you.*
40. Bless the tears, the wet gospel of one sister into another.
41. Bless the unknown.
42. Bless its swarthy, light crunch under foot.
43. Bless the sudden hour.
44. Bless the quiet minute.
45. Bless the spinning second.
46. Bless minutia.
47. Bless the overlooked.
48. Bless the crescendoed whisper calling you home.
49. Bless your new pulse point and the wonder of its music.
50. Bless its seraphic sound, here, after, like a tambourine slapped under river water.
51. Bless the overlooked.
52. Bless even the shadow under the blessing.
53. Bless the heart, that platinum star.
54. Bless its tumble.
55. Bless its spill.
56. Bless its slip.
57. Bless the ache of ache.
58. Bless the coming.
59. Bless the homegoing.
60. Bless the echo: Nia, Nia, Nia.
61. Bless the fleeting.
62. Bless the fleet you join. Nia.
63. Bless your barefoot crossing through the firmament.
64. Bless the months later:
65. Bless the reckoning.
66. Bless the courtroom.
67. Bless the trial.
68. Bless all who suffer the weight of witness.
69. Blessed escape.
70. Blessed sleep.
71. Blessed rest.

72. Bless the wound and the tourniquet.
73. Bless the vanishing cicatrix.
74. Bless it backward from Tifa's neck.
75. Bless it backward from your torso.
76. Bless you whole again.
77. Bless the breath, the breath, the loss, the breath.
78. Bless the broken time.
79. Bless the MacArthur BART Station vigil: the taped posters; scattered lilies and roses; and emptied Henny bottles.
80. Bless the candles melting pools of incarnadine wax on pavement.
81. Bless their Meyer lemon bright sparks.
82. Bless the steady enough hands that light the candles.
83. Bless the flicker, the flicker, the flicker.
84. Bless the thicker fire.
85. Bless the flame that blazes.
86. Bless all that it holds, but does not burn.
87. Bless what it does not burn.
88. Bless the heat.
89. Bless its rise.
90. Bless your ascent. My God.
91. Bless the child.
92. Bless all whom we pull from dirt.
93. Bless an unnamed eternity.
94. Bless this new color of the soul; its mighty incandescence.
95. Bless all whom we hoist high enough to touch the sun.
96. Bless all whom we hoist high enough to be delivered. High enough to be received.
97. Bless this sky. Open.
98. Nia.
99. Nia.
100. Nia.

A NIA FOR AIYANA

for Aiyana Jones

All the goodness in Michigan   rests
                                 in your sole
dimple,   its glisten   and   swirl
like an   onyx   galaxy
                            finding home
            on your face.   Yana,
did you know   that only
1 in 5   people   are born
like this?   Even less
         know   how to smile
like you did—holding   a clod of stars
in your left cheek. Even less
                                could learn
in a lifetime of merely   2,857 days.
A snapshot.
                 A fistful of breaths.
Baby girl, this blessing
          is as short
                     as the archive is hungry
for what remains
unseen. Unbloomed. Unknown.

     What you could have been, Aiyana—
what you could have—

WAHALA: A CURSE HAS MANY HEADS.

One makes me lie prostrate, feigning closed-eye prayers, just to avoid finding out what I've become in the eye of a mirror. One tempts me to say my name backward, like that won't cast a spell that is bone-deep. One makes me sleep with my mouth wide open to the wild thicket on the other side of midnight's lips. One makes me scrape my mother tongue in exchange for the king's language. One makes me think I'm on a first-name basis with him. One makes me think I found salvation in the dying opal glow of my office lightbulb. One makes the stucco ceiling that holds it all in place look like the firmament lowering itself to greet me. One makes me forget that *gift* comes from the same root as the German word for *poison*. One makes me think that if I call money *bread* or *cheese*, that it will be too soft and delicious to choke me. One makes me think that there is a difference between who I am and what I want. One makes me think that the ink of a dollar bill won't seep into me. One makes me think my vision will never fail me, as if I could detect my own blues in the dark. One makes me lie on my side in bed, staring into my skin. I think my flesh, now green, is, by some estimation, a verdant plane. I call myself moss, unaware that this only grows in shady places. By definition, I am a flowerless patch. I rub the mist forming on my arm. I praise myself between heavy eyelids for looking a little like one of God's creations.

IN THE YEAR THAT THE TRASH TOOK ITSELF OUT,

you cleaned up as best you could.

The houseflies, with their forever
devotion to detritus, congregated

at the shore of your mouth. They
waited to catch the bile climbing up

your throat. Swarming around you,
they fed at your lips, until they were

plump, then followed you out of
my living room. You always did

smell like you had something to hide:
when the stench of your apple spice lotion

and hunger lifted from around me,
I learned to taste again. Before I could ask

why you disappeared, I saw a note
on the door: you confessed that God

made a lightning rod of

your intestines every time you smiled
at me while wishing to offer

my breath as hallowed sacrifice to
your wreckage.

SPLIT INFINITY

In autumn, I learn to   forever break bad luck.
As a hand lay on my stomach, I remember what happened
before: the way I was taught
to   soundly build a church from calcified stone.

A hot palm rests on the new danger that slowly bubbles
where the child once was. I sanctuary and begin
to   slightly arc my mouth; it bends the storm
above my head until it makes a haven of its own rain.
My tongue is a plush aisle through which to   gently
lead the holy to the back of my throat.

Three women braid into a wind that rushes me. We bridge
our voices. Opalesce our breaths. This is what we do
to   calmly trouble the water.
We gospel from the base of me until blood spills from
the flesh rock. We loudly echo in my womb. We almost
forget to   quietly watch the way
a broken curse weeps and pleads for mercy.

IN OUR NEW HOME

Our joys are simple and fossilized. While watching
reruns of *Martin*, you and I smack-suck Jolly Ranchers—

watermelons for you, green apples for me. Even after
twenty-two years, we're still catching

up on the episodes we didn't see after he took the Sony 32" to
the curb and, with a hammer, smashed the screen into its own face.

The air is clean here and it is hard not to dance.

In our new home, you water your ferns, once again checking
in on them in Krio: *"Aw di bɔdi?"*

Something is blooming in you.

I hold you here, between my knees and drench your head
with Luster's Pink Oil, part and plait your silver hair. Massage

your scalp until your body is warm and heavy against my leg.
Is warm and heavy. Body. Warm. Heavy.

I gently nudge you and hold the mirror up to your face.
I look over your shoulder to find you, me, and a few of his shards

in the deepest place we can find. We're like that television. Broken
glass that still holds together.

ULOTRICHOUS

After the service in the auditorium, the congregation lines up to greet the pastor, as if he himself were a second coming. Every man is joined to his wife, who is joined to a bonnet, who is joined to a bun, and a bundle of babies. When it's the guest's turn, he cannot control himself. "Your hair, is like Angela Davis's or Colin Kaepernick's—well, which is it?" he asks, as if to quiz her. She smiles instead, taking neither option. "Ulotrichous. That's what they call your hair. It means woolly. Big." She thanks him for the word, for what she knows will be the only gift she will receive. "Where are you from?" "   ," she responds. "Wow, that's tough!" he says, not realizing that she grew up seeing more   than   and never witnessed a   . "It reminds me of growing up in Chicago, my family used to take a couple of kids out of the Robert Taylor Homes every summer to go swimming. It used to be scary walking through those project courtyards. Real scary." *Scary*, she thinks, as she imagines the boys running back to their hell after an afternoon in his. "Bloomington must be hard. Not a good place for people like you." "   ," she retorts, countering his assumption.

But providence, she thinks,
she thinks she says, "But God," she says.
"But God," she says.

It's   well.   I am   well   it is   good   I   am

                        I am   I   am

                        the one   who has   gone

fine   I'm   going,   going   to go   I am   gone

                        going   to   leave

                                                    now.
                                                                you.

I am   going   to   leave.   you   cannot   really   hear

                                                                                  me

screaming: now.   leave   my   hair: me

                                                                                  gone

                                                                                  gone.

disappear.

                                                                        goodbye.

70

DURING LUNCH, MS. ANNE SAYS

Lake Merritt picnic tables, Oakland, CA

have 3, but make sure to space them all apart *carefully*:

by the time your lastborn is somersaulting in your stomach like a medium

load of laundry, your first should already be 4, while your middle child should be 3.

That way, they'll be used to holding each other's hands and yours. No squatting or

lifting for you. You'll hold hands everywhere. When you cross the street. On your way to

the hospital for checkups. And to the delivery room. If he's there, good. If he's not,

that's good, too. Because by then, you will already have months of practice in

the art of clutching and carrying valuables while walking away together.

AUBADE FOR EVERY ROOM IN WHICH MY MOTHER SINGS

"Come celebrate with me that everyday something has tried to kill me and has failed."—*Lucille Clifton*

Before I knew her wail was the key of
Nina Simone's "Don't Let Me Be Misunderstood,"
I called her croon crazy. Thought this
a song I could do nothing with.

*

My mama's bird call is a rusted note grazing
over every portrait of our broken family tree.
It flies through the bedroom door crack to find me
waking in the womb of my sheets.

*

The twist of her brutal cords don't scare me
much anymore, because I've catalogued
each shrill.

*

I know her mouth. Its unrelenting clutch.
How it breaks spells in the name of us
women lost in the forest of sleep.
A bid for us to wake easy.

*

My mama's warble doesn't peck at my
belly anymore. Because I know the words too.
About fire, light, and surrender.

*

Her tongue is a paintbrush tip
stroking Psalms into my skin.
Blessed tincture, she sinks into me.

*

It is 6:00 a.m. and my soul feels an inch
taller and crackles like an old 45.

*

I am ready.

*

There is something in this music for me:

*

Breath.

Selah.

I hear my mama laughing as she kills what
tries to kill us. Slicing shadows that cobweb
our lineage.

She delivers until the whole house rattles;
even the plastic flowers on the mantel break
and weep for mercy.

My mama promises to always feed my
unhinged jaw honey, how I've sprained it
again, mimicking her prayer's jagged plain.

This is how she beckons me to hold this life
with both hands, even when it aches like a
word shunted in bone.

I walk toward the sound of a splinter exiting kin.

Dawn is peeling from dusk. And my mama
is teaching me how to depart from that
which does not love us.

I am spelling my name in my throat.

The glass in my chest expands until it cracks.

She gives me lungs that eat crystal.

A melody rising from the still.

The good sense to make rubble sing.

Today. Today. Today.

NEW AMERICA

Give me a kite that will   twist its   leash in flight to   Oakland's   sapphire expanse.

Give me   tradition   free from the thickness of horror: trick-or-treat without

my mother's   fear of sewing pins and   sedatives nestled in the chocolate's   core. Give us

some good news: an edited issue   of the   *Oakland Tribune* with every splayed corpse

cut from its pages.   Nimble fingers to make   papel picado from newspapers.   Christmas

or Ramadan.   Religion that will not leave me questioned.   A dance and song that

make me too lovable to hurt.   Shears to cut the tightrope umbilical cord.   A flag whose

fabric I can read. Liberty or its synonym.   Give me   smelling salts to

quell   this leg of the Atlantic voyage.   Give me sunscreen   for my face and

arms,   a sturdy cradle rocking   me back and forth   at   the shore of

the Pacific.   A lullaby.   A hush. Whisper with ocean breath that this is   mine.   Give

me a torch to melt all of the pennies   saved to buy this   Volvo   parked in an

immigrant's daydream. Give me an   onyx   Cutlass Supreme blaring Donny Hathaway

from its cushioned innards.   Anthems   to sing   in a language   that I want as

my own.   A Black that is steadfast and opulent.   Which is to say dangerous

and infinite.   Give me a voice   that will not remind my parents of   their homesickness.

Or maybe earplugs,   paper and a pen. Give me a quiet home.   Give me a new

America.   Give our family hands   that aren't scraped   raw by

passport   page edges.   Give me a new America.   Or a new me.   Give me a   land

mass   that reeks of   apple pie and bleach.   A silent pledge of

allegiance.   Give me a license at sixteen.   Wheels and gas   and a hula girl rocking on my

dashboard.   A hail Mary. With no map.   A minute to escape the   sound of my misshapen

name surfing off   the cliff of every tongue.   A minute to drive toward the blue, a

careless twirl toward   where I think I might belong.

FREEBORN

In Krio, there is a word with Atlantic Ocean spray still swirling in its gut:
Freeborn. I heard this word often after dinner was prepared. If, say,

my sister and I couldn't help but shovel soft, clementine-hued heaps
of jollof rice into our mouths on our way to the dining room, my mother

would stop us, demanding that we eat only after sitting at the table. Like
Freeborns. I should tell you that

she would then tuck herself into the corner of the kitchen, standing up,
no sound from her but the harpsichord clink of silverware against plate.

Freeborn—I'd still like to teach her to. Freeborn. Eyes closed, I imagine us
Freeborning somewhere far from this beige bungalow, ripe with the smell of

stewed onions and tomatoes. We Freeborn elsewhere—with a coastal view,
on our beach chair throne. The waves' fangs hungrily rise before us.

Freeborn: I give my mother this old language, watch her grip it between
arthritic fingers, watch her toss the fossilized noun-verb back. Far.

Far enough to hit the water in its tonsils.
Far enough to choke the entire sea.

AMERICAN BEECH

I don't mind when she approaches me, a stranger

on North Walnut Street, who only tells me about what
she sees while reaching two fingers in to retrieve

it from my hair. She squints a bit, fights the menace
of hot, silver, Hoosier sun, and relieves me of a problem

that, for *her*, rests too close to *me*. A deep plunge into
my curls, I wait to see how far she goes, and because I

miss the hands of the women I know, I think I'd even
let her hook her unfamiliar fingers into the lace of my wig,

but she stops short of me feeling completely like home.

It is an American beech leaf, green as green, as opposite of red;
she pulls this weightless raft from inside the crown of me.

In small-town, downtown, there is a woman who does
not know my name, but calls herself my mirror. Haptic grace.

She holds the leaf to my face, then releases it to flow slowly
down the vertical river of air to the pewter concrete. I don't mind

when she approaches me, a stranger on North Walnut Street,

taking a leaf, leaving her fingerprints, to sing and sing and sing
so close to our skin until I hear my own voice say: I feel you, too.

How mighty. The God portal of human touch.

AUNTY X'S DREAM DOOR HAS

A Jimmy proof deadbolt
A knob lock
A door chain
A gaggle of nameless metal parts
        that make biting sounds
A facial detection scanner
A voice recognition device
A crooked LED sign that reads
        "Come back tomorrow"
A chute for strangers that miss the sign
A mailbox for flowers and cards
A sliver of frankincense smoke that
        twirls through its keyhole
Anointed oil blistering the cherry wood
A thick paste made of dead sea mud and
A fistful of rosary beads to cake into
        every opening
        but the peephole and the keyhole
A big enough porch to fit
An armed security guard in front
A medicine man at one side
An oracle on the other and
A preacher behind all three

A table that holds
A plate of jollof rice
A glass of Ribena juice
A broken doorbell and
A key under the mat for
A hungry, dead son to return

home.

AUNTY X BECOMES A UNIT OF LIGHT

While looking in the mirror, my Aunty X surveys her head, wondering if her alopecia has been a lifelong exercise in losing parts of herself. If she's been mourning before she had reason to. She runs four fingers over her collarbone, assessing its dip. A faint protrusion. Not as sunken in as days previous. This is the work of aunties and nieces that have been stuffing her with plantains, rice, plasas, bitter leaf stew, fufu, and all of the delicious fat and starch that round out the sharp angles of a grieving body.

Every hour it seems, they tell her about her hallowed plumpness.
After she awakens from a nap.
After she retrieves mail from the driveway.
Even before the first bite of her next meal.
They sing about the roundness of her face, her chest, her hips, and rear.

Where we come from, this is seen as a type of superpower:
to hold onto fat, especially when struggle tugs at one's bones.

■ ■ ■

Three months before this moment in the mirror, Aunty X sits cross-legged on her neighbor's sun-bleached lawn. The East Oakland autumn heat licks her limbs while the police inspect the perimeter of her home.

Four hours before the moment on the lawn, she loses her voice, its bulbous, magenta casing leaps out of her throat. It explodes and splatters onto the living room walls.

Four seconds before the moment in the living room, she hears the bang and the knock. Ray's last act is to make it to the door. To come inside. As if to return to the womb.

She tries to catch him as he falls toward her, but his weight is too much for her unsteady hands. He lands at her feet, a giant thud.

Aunty X screams so loud, that there is no sound.

Ray deflates. Ray crinkles like the bark of an old tree trunk. Airless grimace. Eternal. This end. Ray enters an ugly kind of sleep.

* * *

The police find the gun in a raspberry puddle next to the front door.

In the first instant, she says that he didn't kill himself.

In the second instant, we wonder who'd planted the gun.

In the third, we realize that there is so much that we do not know.

What we do know: the police inform her that she has to clean the blood, but if she's not able to, they can make referrals.

* * *

When Aunty X isn't sleeping, she is answering the phone.
A call from Freetown. A call from London. A call from Sacramento. A call from Oakland.

A dollop of condolences. Two heaps of questions.
The questions.   The questions.
Who did it?
How do you know?
Did he have enemies?
Did he have demons?
What if they come back?
What if they hunger for more blood?

Are you ready to die, Aunty X?

Most of the aunties and nieces fear retribution; for some time, most disappear.
At least the fridge is full—Aunty X learns to fatten on her own.

■ ■ ■

One morning, Aunty Rosalyn tells Aunty X that she'd seen him
as she poured libations on the porch.

As the golden liquid hit the concrete, he appeared:
Tell my mother that I am sorry, he says, before fading away.

An apology from an apparition.

It takes her months to accept his apology for leaving
blood on her front porch.

Ray is unsure if she loves him in spite of his mistake.
Ray is unsure because she tells every story but the one that is his.

Unsure.
Ray is unable to enter or leave the house.

Ray, a specter living under the doorframe.

■ ■ ■

Sunny, Ray's sister, is perhaps the only one
of Aunty X's three remaining children that she's living for.

Sunny asks: *Why, Ray?*
Sunny asks: *Why lie, ma?*
Sunny asks: *Are you ready to die, too?*

Sunny pries Aunty X's lips open, touches her tongue, this braided pink organ, this lanyard of fables.
Sunny guides Aunty X's hands to her own jaws, swollen and stiffened from the maneuver of protecting
the family's name.

Aunty X is unsure if Sunny loves her in spite of her mistake.

■ ■ ■

In the fourth and final instant, Aunty X tells the truth. She talks about the letter she found in his room, but still can't help but to refer it as "his paper."

Give my girlfriend money for the baby. Give Sunny my speakers, Ray writes.

Aunty X no longer calls it a murder.

And so, Ray enters the front door.

■ ■

Ray takes his seat at the dining table.
He eats the black-eyed peas and
the Sprite Aunty X leaves for him
Though he dies as an adult,
she'll never leave him beer to drink.

Ray is a spirit, but not an elder.

On quiet evenings when she glances at his baby portraits on the wall, she feels him. A small wind surges through her few patches of hair. Her shoulders slacken.

An exhale. A gift. This hereafter.

■ ■ ■

During her break   from college,   Sunny practices   for the

marching band in   the spot   where Ray   shot himself.   There

is a drum   sound that plays   over   the dried blood.

In some world,   this is the closest   a family gets

to recreating

a heartbeat.

. . .

While looking in the mirror, my Aunty X surveys her head, wondering if her alopecia has been a lifelong exercise in losing parts of herself. If she's been mourning before she had reason to. She runs four fingers over her collarbone, assessing its dip. A faint protrusion. Not as sunken in as days previous. This is the work of aunties and nieces that have been stuffing her with plantains, rice, plasas, bitter leaf stew, fufu, and all of the delicious fat and starch that round out the sharp angles of a grieving body.

She ponders the miracle of the bathroom light. All of the lights.
Who paid her bill? She hasn't for months. Or maybe she has.
Yes. Thank you. Yes, she walks, praising in every direction.
Aunty X washes the living room walls with the one million
lumens shooting from her eyes.

Aunty X thanks God for not leaving her in the dark.

■ ■ ■

NOTES

"Eating Malombo Fruit in Freetown, 1989"
    In Sierra Leone, the saba senegalensis is called the malombo fruit.

"Sweet Baby Fabulist"
    Plasas is a type of West African stew often prepared with leafy greens and palm oil.

"Tell Me More, Ms. Angie"
    The Angie Stone quote is sourced from "Angie Stone on Dreams; Bad Habits; Trust Issues and Hate," Thisis50 YouTube Interview, January, 2016.

"A Golden Shovel for My Friend Michael Chan"
    Golden shovel sourced from a line of a Facebook status.

"A Poem for My Uncle"
    This poem is written in the "obverse" form. Created by Nicole Sealey, the "obverse" is a palindrome poem which concludes in a "thesis" question.

"Wahala: A Curse Has Many Heads."
    Meaning "trouble, suffering, or ill-fate," "wahala" is a loan word of probable Hausa origin that is often used in Krio, Sierra Leone's lingua franca.

ACKNOWLEDGMENTS

The author wishes to thank the following journals, magazines, and books in which these poems, sometimes in different versions, first appeared:

The Adroit Journal: "Besaydoo"

Akashic Press: "Repast in the Diversity Center," "Three Days Before My Baptism," "Thurible," and "Pest Control"

Amazon: Day One: "I Ask My Brother Jonathan to Write About Oakland, and He Describes His Room:"

Callaloo, A Journal of African Diaspora Arts and Letters: "Elegy for My Two Step," "In the year that the trash took itself out," and "Metaphors for My Two Step"

Copper Nickel: "Grab Bag (May 1998)"

Entropy: "Rekia and Oscar and All of Their Sky Cousins"

The Journal: "A Golden Shovel for My Friend Michael Chan" and "During lunch, Ms. Anne says"

JuxtaProse: "Listening to Nina Simone Sing 'When Tom Thumb Sings the Blues'"

Ledge Mule Press: "A Haiku for the Bus: 54 Fruitvale BART Station/Merritt College," "Aubade For Every Room in Which My Mother Sings," "Eating Malombo Fruit in Freetown, 1989," "Lessons on Rhotacizing: A Shibboleth," "Oakland as Home. Home as Myth," "Ode," "Resurrection," and "Sweet Baby Fabulist"

Monster House Press Quarterly: "New America"

Oxford Review of Books: "In Our New Home" and "Souvenir"

Meridians: feminism, race, transnationalism: "American Beech"

Nomadic Coffee (California Poets, Volume One): "Le Champ Lexical #1: L'espoir [en 2020 c'est]"

Pleiades: Literature in Context: "A Mouthful"

Pop-Up Magazine: "Soumission Chimique"

Post Road: "Memorializing Nia Wilson: 100 Blessings"

Prairie Schooner: "Marshawn"

Southern Indiana Review: "Wahala: A Curse Has Many Heads"

Vinyl Poetry & Prose: "Mother's Rules"

WusGood.Black: "Haiku Love Letters for Gabby Douglas"

World Literature Today: "Freeborn"

The author also wishes to thank the following publications and anthologies in which several of these poems have been reprinted: *Furious Flower: Seeding the Future of African American Poetry*, *Poetry Daily*, *Poetry Society of America*, and *The Slowdown*.

I am grateful to the Almighty—thank you for the delight, surprise, and mercy you've given me in this life—may I always have the good sense to pay these blessings forward.

I am indebted to the fierce and abiding love of my family—to my grandmother Mrs. Lauretta Cole who prayed for my dreams before I knew what they were; to my mother, Agatha Kamara, the first poet I ever came to know and my greatest muse—thank you for being a constant source of strength and championing who I am and becoming. This win is ours. To my sisters, Mrs. Fatmata Longstreth, Mrs. Kai Clough and Ms. Jenneh Kamara—you're just such a perfect set of sisters for me—I am grateful for your love, candor, humor, and for never leaving me alone. I am grateful that God saw us fit to be each other's each other. To my nephews Kema Clough and Elijah Longsreth—my gorgeous and brilliant boys—you're everything to me and who I do all this for! To my father, Mr. Abu Kamara, it feels right to have you present in this part of the journey. An enormous thank you Professor Michael T. Martin for all you've exemplified for me about the importance of justice, honesty, loyalty, and accountability. Thank you for the delight of kinship and bright, gorgeous, and powerful friendship. I am a better human for it. You've always inspired me to fly high—and so I soar.

To my Aunts: Sylvia Arkaah, Ella Evans, Gloria Jackson, Olive Kwessi, Eyamidé E. Lewis-Coker, Martha Pollett-Coker, Terrie Odabi, Princess Patnelli, Annie Stafford, Yvette Stuart, Olive Yamba, and Palmyra Yamson—thank you for your presence, your support, your encouragement, and your prayers.

To my Uncles: Ivan Cole, Sonny Cole, Bob Heavner, Tokunbo Kayode, Archibald Smith, and Solomon Will—your presences flooded dark spaces with light.

To Milkweed Editions and *Copper Nickel*—and particularly Shannon Blackmer, Yanna Demkiewicz, Katie Hill, Morgan LaRocca, Madi McLaughlin, Wayne Miller, Daniel Slager, Mary Austin Speaker, and Tijqua Daiker, I am thankful for your profound and unparalleled commitment to the realization of this book. I am deeply moved by your labor, vision, generosity, patience, and brilliance. To Bailey Hutchinson, my infinite gratitude for your attentiveness, care, and ability to hear every note that each word has to sing!

To Professor Amaud Jamaul Johnson—thank you for your writing that endows the world with dignity, candor, and light. I am endlessly humbled by your belief in this book, its messages, its visions, its hopes and its wishes. From Oakland to Compton and every body of water and land in between—this is your book, too.

To Professor Wayne Miller of the University of Colorado, Boulder and *Copper Nickel*—thank you for your overall championing of poetry, and your guidance and generosity of spirit with *Besaydoo*. Your encouragement, by way of counsel and celebration, has been an incredible source of upliftment in my bookmaking and publishing journey. To Professor Ross Gay—thank you for continuing to evidence that luminous writers can also be luminous human beings! I am deeply grateful for your kinship, guidance, creativity, and kindness.

I would like to thank the faculty, staff, and my peers in the English Department of the College of Arts and Sciences of the University of Cincinnati for your artistic and intellectual support and fostering of creativity.

I extend my most heartfelt gratitude to Professor Jenn Glaser—from my first day at the University of Cincinnati to the completion of my dissertation, your mentorship, wisdom, knowledge, compassion, and friendship have been such rich sources of strength and inspiration. I am so incredibly grateful for your guidance and encouragement, without which my PhD would have never been completed with success. I adore you and thank you endlessly.

To Provost Valerio Ferme—thank you for your support of, and attention to, my artistic and academic progress during my doctoral studies and beyond. Your time and investment have been instrumental in my journey!

To my dissertation committee members, Professor Jenn Glaser, Professor John Drury, Professor Eileen Julien, and Professor Felicia Zamora: my work is a product of your brilliance, honesty, instruction, and kindness—there are no greater gifts.

A special thanks to Jenny Lin and Jenn Habel for your steadfast support along the years. You kept me afloat in more ways than I can express!

To my blood and chosen family and friends: Alex Abreu, Allison Adair, Joshua Aiken, Raúl Alcantar, Elsa Alibert, The Amao-L'Hour Family, Clyde Allen, Stine An, Kelly Armstrong, Ellen Austin-Li, Danielle Barrios, Vanessa Barrios, Jessica Ballard, Ellen Bass, Tyler Batson, Bel Beeson, Anya Black, Grover Black, The Black Family, Dr. Regina Bradley, Holly Brians Ragusa, Justin Brookhart, Devin Bustin, Dr. Taylor Byas, The Byrd Family, Dr. Marianne Chan, Michael Chan, Alison Chang, Angela Chang, Antoine Chardayre, Becca Chase-Chen, Aminah Cherry, Jamilah Cherry, Lauran Cherry, Jeff Clough, Janderson Coswosk, Justin Counts, Kasa Cotugno, Justin Counts, Híl Davis, Ajanaé Dawkins, Dr. Cara Dees, Anni Domingo, Mitchell Douglas, Morgan Eldridge, Christina Eskridge, The Essakalli-Klear Family, Meghann Farnsworth, Jamie Farris, Luca Fitzgerald, Dr. Terry Flennaugh, Michael Frazier, Bix Gabriel, Jorge Garcia, Julien Germain-Rutherford, John Gibson, Max Gibson, Kris Gillis, Dr. Joanne Godley, Elena Estella Green, Mary Green, Kari Gunter-Seymour, Dr. Sarah Haak, Pauletta Hansel, Dick Hague, Bob Heavner, Rachel Heavner, Kyle Heckler, Sister Maureen Hester, Dr. Sakinah Hofler, Dr. Vanessa Holden, Jon Holland, Myla Hollyfield, Desirae Hosley, Scott Holzman, Dr. Emma Hudelson, Libby Hunter, Dr. Manuel Iris, Brandon Isaac, Noor Jaber, Jamie Jackson, Marlin Jenkins, Dee Johnson, Dr. Janine Joseph, Jeremy Jusek, Allison Kephart, Alyssa Konermann, Ben Kline, Julian Koroma, Lisa Kwong, Liz Latty, Maurisa Li-A-Ping, Alicia Link, Michael Link, Kelly Lloyd, Mariama Lockington, Antonio López, Dr. Lisa Low, Benoît Luce, Wendy Lumsdaine, Elaine Olund, Tracy Mahon, Zainab Mansaray-During, Amanda Meth, Dr. Brittney Miles, Ciara Miller, Dr. Nicholas Molbert, David Moody, Rachel Naor, Kierra Newman, Christine Nguyen, Hafizah Omar, Jim Palmarini, Apollo Papafrangou, Wendell Pascual, Hazel Pegues Williams, Dr. Gabriel Peoples, Dr. Michael Peterson, Pamela Pinnock, Jesus Portillo, Jim Purcell, Tamara Ramey-Carter, Emma Raynor, Laura Raynor, Molly Raynor, Ken Raynor, L. Renée, Dr. Hannah Rice, Jake Riordan, Ahely Rios, Dr. Sam Ritter, Bre Robinson, Dr. Cristy Robinson, Amy Roche, Cedric Rose, Joe Samalin, Dr. Simone Savannah, Nathan Schwarzendruber, David Selestok, Amare Shaw, Dr. Samyak Shertok, Jenna Harvey Sinclair, Keith and Liz Sloan, Stephanie Smith, Chinzalée Sonami, Laetitia Sonami, Rosetta Springer, Michael Starks, Aaron Stein, Daniel "Sully" Sullivan, Dr. Thea Quiray Tagle, Adam Tapia-Grassi, Colette Taylor-Jones, Dave Torneo, Sharita Towne, Dacha Tran, Dr. Tiffany Tucker, José Vadi, Melissa Vogley-Woods, Christopher Wang, Abby Wheeler, Dr. Chelsea Whitton, Kara Willis, Dr. Maddy Wattenberg, David Watters, Dick Westheimer, Sam Weiss and The Weiss Family, Andrea Welton, Marcus Wicker, The Wright Family, CJ Wooten, Dr. Matthew Yeager, Biz Young,

Jakki Young, Kayte Young, Dr. Mark Youssef, and Jacob Zimmerman—thank you for the gifts of upliftment, friendship, and kinship. Your light pulls me through.

To 826 Valencia, the Academy of American Poets, African Poetry Book Fund, Akashic Books, the Black Film Center/Archive, Le Collège, Le Lycée, et L'université Blaise Pascal, BLINK Cincinnati, Busboys and Poets, the City of Cincinnati Office of the Mayor Aftab Pureval, the College of Arts and Sciences Humanities Institute of Indiana University, Bloomington, the Callaloo Creative Writing Workshop, the Cincinnati and Hamilton County Public Library, the Creole Heritage Organization of California, the Critical Poetics Research Group of Nottingham Trent University, Geraldine R. Dodge Poetry Program, Dohn Community High School, Dr. Brian Taylor and Every Nation Cincinnati, FotoFocus Cincinnati, Amanda Uhle and The Hawkins Project, Head-Royce School, Holy Names University, Hughes STEM High School, Indiana University, Bloomington, Professor Eleanor Henderson and the Writing Department of Ithaca College, the *Kenyon Review* Adult Writers Workshop, Ledge Mule Press, John Faherty and the Mercantile Library, Professor Ginetta Candelario and *Meridians: feminism, race, transnationalism* of Smith College, Middlebury College, the Ohio Poetry Association, The Oxbow School, the Philanthropic Educational Organization, Rev. Dr. Bruce R. Rose and Second Baptist Church, the National Book Critics Circle, the Taft Research Center of University of Cincinnati, the Vermont Studio Center, The Well, WordPlay Cincy, the University of California, Riverside, Xavier University, the Yates Fellowship Program of the University of Cincinnati, and Youth Speaks—thank you to these institutions and key individuals within these institutions for providing me with critical and necessary and safe spaces to learn, to teach, and to realize my creative, intellectual, and spiritual formations.

To educators: Professor Chris Abani, Dr. Elizabeth Alexander, Professor Chris Bachelder, Professor Michelle Bloom, Professor Stacey Lynn Brown, Professor Jane Bryce, Nínive Calegari, Dean Christopher Carter, Mr. Ernie Chen, Professor Kwame Dawes, Professor Russel Durst, Professor Christine Duvergé, Mr. Dave Eggers, Provost Valerio Ferme, Mrs. Phyllis Forsyth, Professor Faye Gleisser, Professor Peter Gil-Sheridan, Mrs. Margaret Gill, Professor Aracelis Girmay, Professor Vivian Halloran, Mr. Alex Harp, Mrs. Judy Harrison, Mrs. Mabel Haskins, Professor Juan Felipe Herrera, Professor James Lee, Professor Rebecca Lindenberg, Professor Adrian Matejka, Mr. Howard McCoy, Professor Audrey McCluskey, Professor Alyce Miller, Ms. Alison Park, Mr. Peter Reinke, Professor Micheline Rice-Maximin, Ms. Marilyn Russell, Professor Maurya Simon, Mr. Andy Spear, Professor Leah Stewart, Mr. Carl Thiermann, Mr. Stephen Thomas, Professor Jacinda Townsend, and Professor Dwight Yates—thank you for your challenge, care, and belief in me.

To the sweet, brilliant, and enduring memory of my sister Chanel Andrea Selestok, my oldest and dearest friend on Earth. May the words in these pages evidence your unique and perfect understanding of love and all that you still teach me about the miracle of it.

To the gorgeous legacy of Jake Adam York, his personhood and art. In this season, I continue to learn the ways his spirit rises from the soul soil of everyone he touched. Forever in bloom. In bloom. In bloom.

JP Leong

YALIE SAWEDA KAMARA is the author of *Besaydoo*, winner of the 2023 Jake Adam York Prize. She is a Sierra Leonean American writer, educator, and researcher from Oakland, California, and the 2022–2023 Cincinnati and Mercantile Library Poet Laureate. A 2023 Academy of American Poets Poet Laureate Fellow, she has received fellowships from the Vermont Studio Center, the National Book Critics Circle, and *Callaloo*. Kamara's poetry, fiction, interviews, and translations have been published in *The Adroit Journal*, *Callaloo*, *Black Camera*, *Puerto del Sol*, and elsewhere. She is the Director of Creative Youth Leadership at WordPlay Cincy and is an Adjunct Assistant Professor at the University of Cincinnati.

The Jake Adam York Prize for a first or second collection of poems was established in 2016 to honor the name and legacy of Jake Adam York (1972–2012). York was the founder of *Copper Nickel*, a nationally distributed literary journal at the University of Colorado Denver. His work as a poet and scholar explored memory and social history, and particularly the Civil Rights Movement.

The judge for the 2023 Jake Adam York Prize was Amaud Jamaul Johnson.

milkweed
EDITIONS

Founded as a nonprofit organization in 1980, Milkweed Editions is an independent publisher.
Our mission is to identify, nurture, and publish transformative literature,
and build an engaged community around it.

Milkweed Editions is based in Bdé Óta Othúŋwe (Minneapolis) within Mní Sota Makhóčhe, the traditional homeland of the Dakhóta people. Residing here since time immemorial, Dakhóta people still call Mní Sota Makhóčhe home, with four federally recognized Dakhóta nations and many more Dakhóta people residing in what is now the state of Minnesota. Due to continued legacies of colonization, genocide, and forced removal, generations of Dakhóta people remain disenfranchised from their traditional homeland. Presently, Mní Sota Makhóčhe has become a refuge and home for many Indigenous nations and peoples, including seven federally recognized Ojibwe nations. We humbly encourage our readers to reflect upon the historical legacies held in the lands they occupy.

milkweed.org

Milkweed Editions, an independent nonprofit publisher, gratefully acknowledges sustaining support from our Board of Directors; the Alan B. Slifka Foundation and its president, Riva Ariella Ritvo-Slifka; the Amazon Literary Partnership; *Copper Nickel*; the McKnight Foundation; the National Endowment for the Arts; the National Poetry Series; and other generous contributions from foundations, corporations, and individuals. Also, this activity is made possible by the voters of Minnesota through a Minnesota State Arts Board Operating Support grant, thanks to a legislative appropriation from the arts and cultural heritage fund. For a full listing of Milkweed Editions supporters, please visit milkweed.org.

Interior design by Tijqua Daiker
Typeset in Jenson

Adobe Jenson was designed by Robert Slimbach for Adobe
and released in 1996. Slimbach based Jenson's roman styles
on a text face cut by fifteenth-century type designer Nicolas Jenson,
and its italics are based on type created by Ludovico Vicentino
degli Arrighi, a late fifteenth-century papal scribe
and type designer.